REALLY WEIRD ANIMALS

BUTTERFLIES AND MOTHS

CLARE HIBBERT

W
FRANKLIN WATTS
LONDON • SYDNEY

First published in 2011 by Franklin Watts

Copyright © 2011 Arcturus Publishing Limited

Franklin Watts
338 Euston Road
London NW1 3BH

Franklin Watts Australia
Level 17/207 Kent Street, Sydney NSW 2000

Produced by Arcturus Publishing Limited,
26/27 Bickels Yard, 151–153 Bermondsey Street, London SE1 3HA

The right of Clare Hibbert to be identified as the author of this work has been asserted by her in accordance with the Copyright, Designs and Patents Act 1988.

Series concept: Discovery Books Ltd, 2 College Street, Ludlow, Shropshire SY8 1AN
www.discoverybooks.net

Managing editor: Paul Humphrey
Editor and picture researcher: Clare Hibbert
Design: sprout.uk.com

Photo acknowledgements: Corbis: pp 5 (Visuals Unlimited), 9t (Volkmar Brockhaus), 11t (Naturfoto Honal), 15b (Gavriel Jecan), 19r (Frans Lanting), 20 (Roy Morsch), 25t (Frans Lanting), 26t (Visuals Unlimited), 27t (Darrell Gulin/Science Faction); FLPA: cover and pp 1 (Richard Becker), 4 (Rolf Nussbaumer/Imagebroker), 12t (Malcolm Schuyl), 12b (Ingo Arndt/Minden Pictures), 23b (Malcolm Schuyl), 28b (Fabio Pupin), 29 (Fabio Pupin); iStockphoto: pp 6t (jeridu), 8 (U-photo), 10 (fasloof), 14r (tomh1000), 22 (TranceDrumer), 23t (MorganLeFaye), 25bl (Atelopus), 31 (MorganLeFaye); Oxford Scientific Films: pp 11b (David Fox), 15t (David M Dennis); Photolibrary: pp 13 (Paul Beard), 27b (Satyendra Tiwari/Oxford Scientific), 28t (Oxford Scientific); Shutterstock: pp 3 (James Laurie), 6b (Ivan Hor), 7 (Jeff Grabert), 9b (vblinov), 14l (James Laurie), 16 (WitR), 17tr (Cathy Keifer), 17bl (Cathy Keifer), 18t (Melinda Fawver), 18bl (Cathy Keifer), 18br (Cathy Keifer), 19t (James Laurie), 21t (Alex James Bramwell), 21b (Ziga Camernik), 24t (Mircea Bezergheanu), 24b (Mircea Bezergheanu), 26b (Cathy Keifer), 32 (Cathy Keifer).

Cover picture: A male lobster moth, Wales, UK.

The website addresses (URLs) included in the resources section on page 31 were valid at the time of going to press. However, because of the nature of the Internet, it is possible that some addresses may have changed, or the sites may have changed or closed down since publication. While the author, packager and publisher regret any inconvenience this may cause to readers, no responsibility for any such changes can be accepted by the author, packager or publisher.

Every attempt has been made to clear copyright. Should there be any inadvertent omission, please apply to the publisher for rectification.

A CIP catalogue record for this book is available from the British Library.

Dewey Decimal Classification Number 595.7'89

ISBN 978 1 4451 0522 2

Printed in China

Franklin Watts is a division of Hachette Children's Books, an Hachette UK company.
www.hachette.co.uk

CONTENTS

CECROPIA MOTH

This moth looks like it's wearing a feather headdress! The cecropia moth is North America's largest moth, and those 'feathers' are its bushy antennae, or feelers.

Like all moths, the cecropia moth uses its antennae to sniff out food and mates.

Moths and butterflies start life as larvae (caterpillars). Caterpillars moult as they grow, losing their outer skin.

A newly-hatched cecropia moth caterpillar is small, black and hairy. After a couple of moults, its body is green with orange and blue knobbly bits!

WEIRD OR WHAT?

Squirrels are bad news for cecropia moths. They snack on their pupae.

The cecropia moth caterpillar goes through four moults, then becomes a pupa. While it is a pupa, it changes into its adult form.

CECROPIA MOTH FACTS

SIZE: wingspan of around 13 cm
HOME: North America
EATS: leaves, eg maple, cherry and birch (larvae)

This butterfly flying in to feed at a flower is a golden birdwing. Birdwings include the largest butterflies and come in all the colours of the rainbow.

Birdwing Butterfly

Birdwings live in tropical Asia and Australia. The Rajah Brooke's birdwing flutters through Indonesian rainforests. Its leaf-green wings help it to blend in.

WEIRD OR WHAT?

The world's largest butterfly is a birdwing – the Queen Alexandra's birdwing. The female can have a wingspan of 30 centimetres or more.

The Cairns birdwing is Australia's largest butterfly. This one is resting on a leaf. When the butterfly lands on a flower, it can uncurl its long mouthpart to suck up nectar.

BIRDWING BUTTERFLY FACTS

SIZE: wingspan of 15-30 cm
HOME: tropical rainforests, Asia, Australasia
EATS: leaves of vines (larvae); nectar (adults)

GLASSWING BUTTERFLY

SIZE: wingspan of about 6 cm
HOME: Central and South America
EATS: cestrum leaves (larvae);
nectar (adults)

The glasswing butterfly has see-through windows on its wings!

Most butterfly wings are covered with coloured scales. Some parts of the glasswing's wings do not have these, so they appear see-through.

WEIRD OR WHAT?

Glasswing caterpillars feed on cestrum plants. They take in toxins from the leaves that make them poisonous to predators.

Plume Moth

The plume moth wins the prize for the weirdest wings. Each wing has a long, thin support with feathery 'plumes' trailing off it. It looks like the spooky ghost of a moth.

WEIRD OR WHAT?

Plume moths roll up their wings when they are resting.

PLUME MOTH FACTS

SIZE: wingspan of about 3 cm
HOME: grasslands, gardens, worldwide
EATS: leaves and shoots (larvae); nectar (adults)

All moths have leg spurs, but these are especially noticeable in plume moths. The moth uses the spurs to groom its antennae.

ATLAS MOTH

ATLAS MOTH FACTS

SIZE: wingspan of 25 cm or more
HOME: tropical and subtropical forests,
South-East Asia
EATS: evergreen leaves (larvae)

The handsome atlas moth has the biggest wings of any moth. Because of this, it finds it difficult to fly.

WEIRD OR WHAT?

Adult atlas moths survive on fat stores they laid down as caterpillars. Since they do not eat, they do not have proper mouthparts.

BURNET MOTH

Burnet moths are active during the day. Their bright colours warn predators that they are poisonous.

Peekaboo! Who's coming out of this pupa? Those long antennae belong to a wasp, not a burnet moth.

BURNET MOTH FACTS

SIZE: wingspan of 2.5-4 cm
HOME: temperate and tropical regions worldwide
EATS: bird's-foot trefoil (larvae); nectar (adults)

WEIRD OR WHAT?

Some wasp parasites lay their eggs inside burnet moth pupae. When they hatch, the wasp grubs feed on caterpillar meat.

PUSS MOTH

WEIRD OR WHAT?

The puss moth caterpillar's head has an extra defensive feature – it can squirt out formic acid.

Just like its namesake, the cat, an adult puss moth has a furry body.

This caterpillar has a ring around its head with two false eyes. These features make the puss moth caterpillar look like a much bigger animal, and confuse predators.

PUSS MOTH FACTS

SIZE: wingspan of 6 cm or more
HOME: woodlands, Europe, North Africa
EATS: willow and aspen leaves (larvae);
       nectar (adults)

Owl Butterfly

WEIRD OR WHAT?

Male owl butterflies hold flying competitions. The females mate with the most talented fliers.

'Twit-twoo!' The owl butterfly is named for the huge eyespots on its wings, which look like owls' eyes.

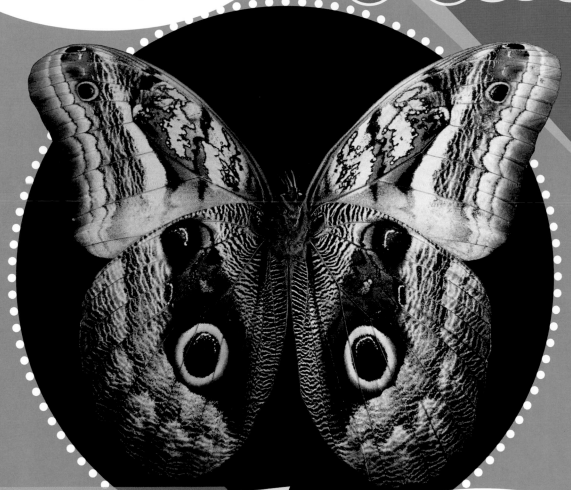

OWL BUTTERFLY FACTS

SIZE: wingspan up to 14 cm
HOME: tropical rainforests, Central and South America
EATS: leaves (larvae); juice of rotting fruit (adults)

Most butterflies are active in the day, but the owl butterfly feeds at dusk, when there are fewer birds around that might eat it.

WEIRD OR WHAT?

Male swallowtails sometimes suck up muddy water – for the useful salts it contains. They will also occasionally drink urine or feed on dung. How revolting!

With its black-and-yellow stripes, it is no surprise that this butterfly is known as a tiger swallowtail.

Swallowtails are named for their pointed back wings, which are shaped like a swallow's tail. The largest species is this giant swallowtail.

Swallowtail caterpillars use camouflage to stay safe. Many young ones look like bird droppings.

When they get bigger, the caterpillars' eyespots make them look like a scary snake.

SWALLOWTAIL BUTTERFLY FACTS

SIZE: wingspan up to 14 cm
HOME: woodlands, North and Central America
EATS: leaves (larvae); nectar (adults)

PALE TUSSOCK MOTH

Is this a caterpillar or a feather duster? With its tufty-haired body, the pale tussock moth caterpillar is hard to beat for all-out weirdness.

WEIRD OR WHAT?

Don't get too close to this caterpillar. Brushing against its poison-tipped hairs can give you a nasty rash.

PALE TUSSOCK MOTH FACTS

SIZE: wingspan of around 5 cm
HOME: woodlands, Europe
EATS: leaves, eg oak, birch, lime and hop (larvae)

The adult moth is far less fancy. Its colouring and markings blend in with its surroundings.

LUNA MOTH

'Luna' means moon. Luna moths are more active at night than during the day.

WEIRD OR WHAT?

A female luna moth lays up to 300 eggs. She lays just five on each leaf, so the caterpillars will have enough food.

LUNA MOTH FACTS

SIZE: wingspan up to 11.5 cm
HOME: North America
EATS: leaves, eg alder, birch and hickory (larvae)

The adult stage of the luna moth's life lasts about a week. The male relies on its sensitive antennae to locate a female to mate with.

The monarch butterfly caterpillar's bold stripes warn predators to steer clear. It feeds only on the leaves and flowers of the poisonous milkweed plant.

MONARCH BUTTERFLY

Inside this hard, shiny case, or chrysalis, a monarch caterpillar's body is breaking down into mush, then being rebuilt into an adult butterfly. This is how all butterflies change, and it is called metamorphosis.

After about 10 days, the chrysalis turns from milky to clear. The butterfly begins to break free.

The adult butterfly sucks up nectar with its long mouthpart, which is like a drinking straw.

MONARCH BUTTERFLY FACTS

SIZE: wingspan around 9 cm
HOME: mostly North and Central America
EATS: milkweed (larvae); nectar (adults)

Monarchs spend the winter in California and Mexico. They cluster on fir trees in a kind of hibernation.

WEIRD OR WHAT?

Monarchs are masters of migration. They can fly as far as 4,750 kilometres in a year.

In spring, the butterflies head back to northern North America, and the life cycle begins all over again.

Tent Moth

This silken structure is a nest built by tent moth caterpillars. They rest when they are not feeding. These monstrous munchers are pests that can strip whole forests.

WEIRD OR WHAT?

A female tent moth may fly hundreds of kilometres to lay her eggs, looking for somewhere with enough food to feed her hungry caterpillars.

DEATH'S-HEAD HAWK MOTH

This moth's spooky name comes from the marking on its body. It looks like a human skull!

WEIRD OR WHAT?

Death's-head hawk moths can mimic the scent of bees. They do this so they can burgle beehives for honey without the bees noticing.

DEATH'S-HEAD HAWK MOTH FACTS

SIZE: wingspan of 12 cm
HOME: Europe, North Africa, Asia
EATS: leaves (larvae); honey (adults)

This is a death's-head hawk moth caterpillar. If disturbed, it makes a clicking noise.

MORPHO BUTTERFLY

Gorgeous or what?
This beautiful butterfly is a blue
morpho. Its jewel-like colour
is not caused by blue pigment.
It is a trick of the light.

The wings are
covered in millions of tiny
scales that reflect back more
than two-thirds of the light
that falls on them.

MORPHO BUTTERFLY FACTS

SIZE: wingspan of 7.5-20 cm
HOME: rainforests, Central and South America
EATS: leaves (larvae); sap, juice of rotting fruit (adults)

When a blue morpho is resting, it may close its wings to reveal their dull, brown underside. They have eyespots that make them appear to be a much bigger animal and help to put off predators.

These caterpillars appear to be snuggling up, but morphos should beware of their brothers and sisters – they're cannibals!

WEIRD OR WHAT?

The eyes of morpho butterflies are very sensitive to light. They can see each other over long distances because their wings bounce back so much light.

HUMMINGBIRD HAWK MOTH

The hummingbird hawk moth is famous for its super-fast wing beat. The rapid movement makes the wings 'hum' – just like a hummingbird's.

This moth feeds like a hummingbird, too. It uses its long mouthpart to reach deep inside flowers for nectar.

HUMMINGBIRD HAWK MOTH FACTS

SIZE: wingspan up to 4.5 cm
HOME: Europe, North Africa, Asia
EATS: leaves (larvae); nectar (adults)

WEIRD OR WHAT?

Hummingbird hawk moths return to the same flowerbeds at the same time each day.

Giddy-up! This caterpillar looks like it is wearing a horse's saddle! No wonder it is called the saddleback moth.

SADDLEBACK MOTH

Watch out for the saddleback's hairs. They can give you a nasty sting that leaves a rash on your skin for days.

WEIRD OR WHAT?

The saddleback caterpillar has a pair of fleshy horns at either end of its body. These confuse predators, as they do not know which end to attack.

SADDLEBACK MOTH FACTS

SIZE: wingspan around 3.5 cm
HOME: North America
EATS: leaves from woody shrubs (larvae)

Regal Moth

'Regal' means kingly – and with its grand, showy colours, this large moth certainly looks rather royal.

REGAL MOTH FACTS

SIZE: wingspan up to 15.5 cm
HOME: woodlands, North America
EATS: leaves of nut trees (larvae)

WEIRD OR WHAT?

Regal moths pupate (turn into a pupa) in an underground burrow, rather than a cocoon.

Its caterpillars are nicknamed hickory horned devils. One of their favourite foods are leaves from hickory trees.

When its wings are closed, the orange oak leaf butterfly looks just like a dead leaf. What brilliant camouflage!

WEIRD OR WHAT?

Orange oak leafs that come out of their pupal stage during the rainy season have stronger colouring than dry-season butterflies.

ORANGE OAK LEAF BUTTERFLY

ORANGE OAK LEAF BUTTERFLY FACTS

SIZE: wingspan around 7.5 cm
HOME: tropics, Asia
EATS: leaves (larvae);
       nectar (adults)

The butterfly is easier to see with its wings open.

Silk Moth

Silk for clothes comes from the silk moth. Most moth caterpillar species produce silk for their cocoons, but the silk moth's threads are so super-fine that people harvest them to make silk cloth.

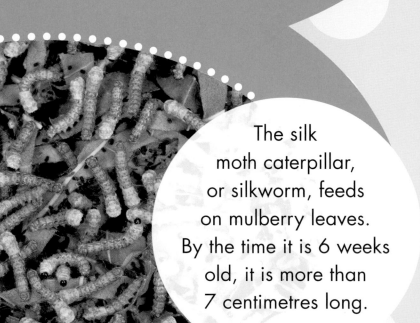

The silk moth caterpillar, or silkworm, feeds on mulberry leaves. By the time it is 6 weeks old, it is more than 7 centimetres long.

To spin its cocoon, it pushes out one strand of silk from its spinneret. This single thread may be nearly a kilometre long.

The Chinese have been farming silkworms for nearly 5,000 years. They kept how to do it a closely-guarded secret!

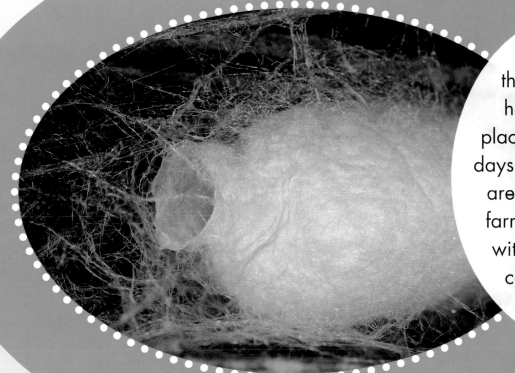

In the wild, the cocoon would have been a safe place to pupate. These days, the only silkworms are farmed ones. The farmer kills the pupae with hot steam, then collects the silken cocoons.

The farmer does allow some of the silk moths to pupate. They will produce the next generation of silkworms.

SILK MOTH FACTS

SIZE: wingspan up to 5 cm
HOME: native to China, now raised worldwide
EATS: mulberry leaves (larvae)

REALLY WEIRD ANIMALS

antenna (plural antennae) One of a pair of feelers on an insect's head, used to smell, touch and hear.

camouflage Colours or patterns that help an animal to blend in to the surrounding environment.

cannibal An animal that eats others of its species.

chrysalis A hard case that protects the pupa of a butterfly or moth.

cocoon A soft, silken case that protects the pupa of a butterfly or moth.

eyespot A marking that resembles the eye of a larger animal, and deters predators.

hibernation A period of time when an animal's body slows right down, in a kind of sleep.

larva (plural larvae) The young stage of an animal, usually an insect. The larva looks different to its adult form.

life cycle All the stages in the life of a living thing, for example from egg to caterpillar to butterfly.

metamorphosis The change from one form to another.

migration A regular journey that an animal makes at the same time each year, for example to feeding or breeding grounds.

moult To lose skin, hair or an outer casing. Caterpillars moult as they grow.

nectar A sweet substance produced by flowers to encourage pollinating animals, such as insects.

parasite A living thing that does not produce or find its own food, but instead lives on a host that it relies on for food.

pigment Colouring.

plume A trailing feather or feather-like structure.

predator An animal that hunts and kills other animals for food.

pupa (plural pupae) The stage in an insect's life when it changes from one form to another, for example from a soft-bodied caterpillar to a winged butterfly.

rainforest A forest habitat where rain falls almost every day. In a tropical rainforest, the climate is hot and steamy all year round.

scale One of the thin, flat plates that cover the wings of a butterfly or moth and give it its colour.

species One particular type of living thing. Members of the same species look similar and can reproduce together in the wild.

spinneret A silk-producing organ, found under a caterpillar's head.

spur A spike sticking out from the leg.

subtropical Describes the regions of the earth that lie between the tropics and the poles, where the climate is warm in summer and cool in winter.

temperate From the two regions of the earth that lie between the equator (the imaginary line that circles the middle of the earth) and the poles, where the climate is warm in summer and cold in winter.

toxin A poison.

tropical Describes the warm, wet part of the world near to the equator.

wingspan The distance from wing tip to wing tip when a butterfly or moth opens its wings.

FURTHER INFORMATION

Books

Amazing Animals: Butterflies by Edward S Barnard (Gareth Stevens Publishing, 2008)

Butterfly: A Photographic Portrait by Thomas Marent (Dorling Kindersley, 2008)

DK Science: Buzz by Caroline Bingham, Ben Morgan and Matthew Robertson (Dorling Kindersley, 2007)

Extreme Insects by Richard Jones (Collins, 2010)

The Secret Lives of Backyard Bugs by Judy Burris and Wayne Richards (Storey Publishing, 2011)

DVDs

David Attenborough's Life in the Undergrowth (2 Entertain Video, 2005)

Natural History: Insects and Arachnids (www.a2zcds, 2007)

Websites

Butterfly Conservation
www.butterfly-conservation.org

Butterfly Metamorphosis
http://lifecycle.onenessbecomesus.com/

The Children's Butterfly Site
www.kidsbutterfly.org

National Geographic: Monarch Butterfly
http://animals.nationalgeographic.com/
bugs/monarch-butterfly/

Natural History Museum: Butterflies and
Moths of the World
www.nhm.ac.uk/research-curation/
research/projects/butmoth/

INDEX